LIBRARY OF WEIRD

THE WORLD'S
WEIRDEST
ANIMALS

by Lindsy O'Brien

raintree

a Capstone company — publishers for children

Raintree is an imprint of Capstone Global Library Limited, a company incorporated in England and Wales having its registered office at 7 Pilgrim Street, London, EC4V 6LB – Registered company number: 6695582

www.raintree.co.uk
myorders@raintree.co.uk

ISBN 978 1 4062 9205 3
18 17 16 15 14
10 9 8 7 6 5 4 3 2 1

British Library Cataloguing in Publication Data
A full catalogue record for this book is available from the British Library.

Editorial Credits
Aaron Sautter, editor; Kyle Grenz, designer; Charmaine Whitman and Katy LaVigne, production designers; Pam Mitsakos, media researcher; Kathy McColley, production specialist

Photo Credits
Dreamstime: Smellme, 10; Getty Images: Photodisc, 29 (bottom); Minden Pictures: Norbert Wu, 17; Nature Picture Library: Solvin Zankl, 16; Newscom: "CMSP Biology", 11, Minden Pictures/FLPA/Dembinsky Photo Ass, 8, ZUMAPRESS/Kerryn Parkinson, 13, Visual&Written, 15; Shutterstock: BMJ, 21, Erni, 29 (top), gallimaufry, 7, Sue Green, 26, Arto Hakola, 9, cover, Eric Isselee, 5, Nataly Karol, 18, Steve Lovegrove, back cover, Molly Marshall, 25, Dudarev Mikhail, 19, 24, nattanan726, 27, orlandin, 14, Yakov Oskanov, 6, Peter Reijners, 23, reptiles4all, 28, Michael Wiggenhauser, 20; Wikimedia:Darron Birgenheier, 22

Design Elements
Shutterstock: AridOcean, KID_A (throughout)

Printed in China.

CONTENTS

WEIRD AND WACKY
ANIMALS

Have you heard about fish that look like blobs of goo or glow like torches? Have you seen the antelope that can stand on their hind legs? What about a chicken that looks like it should be wearing a scarf?

From insects to birds, animals around the world have a wide variety of weird characteristics. Some animals look strange, while others display bizarre behaviour. But being different often helps these animals to survive in the wild. Some animals have bright colours or act strangely to scare away **predators**. Other animals have odd body shapes that help them to get food that others can't reach.

predator *animal that hunts other animals for food*

Weird animals are found around the world. From the air, to the land, to the sea, and even in space, outlandish creatures can be found wherever you look. Get ready to meet some crazy creatures that you have to see to believe.

OKAPI

Okapis are distant relatives of giraffes. Though smaller, they have a similar body shape to giraffes. But unlike giraffes, these animals have zebra-like stripes on their hindquarters and front legs. Okapis have tongues that are up to 36 centimetres long. They use their long tongues to grab leaves and shoots from tall branches. Okapis are rarely seen in the wild. For a long time people thought these animals were a myth. For this reason they were given the nickname "African unicorns".

CHAPTER 1

MYSTERIOUS MAMMALS

You may already be familiar with many mammals. Common animals such as cats, dogs, foxes and horses are all mammals. But some of the world's weirdest animals are mammals too.

FLYING FOX

The flying fox isn't a fox at all – it's a bat! But its furry face and big eyes make it look like a fox. Most bats eat insects, but flying foxes are **vegetarians**. They feed on **nectar**, pollen and fruit. Flying foxes live in several tropical areas around the world.

SAIGA ANTELOPE

Saiga antelope roam the plains of Central Asia. These animals once had a population of millions, but today there are only about 150,000 of them in the wild. Saiga antelopes have large humped noses that help to control the temperature of the air they breathe. This ability helps the animals to survive extreme hot and cold temperatures during summer and winter.

TARSIER

Tarsiers live in South-East Asia. These small creatures grow to about 10 to 15 centimetres long. They eat mostly insects, but sometimes they eat lizards or small birds as well. Tarsiers have giant eyes that help them to see their prey in the dark. These creatures can also turn their heads half way around their bodies to see what's directly behind them!

mammal *warm-blooded animal that gives birth to live young and feeds them with milk*

vegetarian *animal or person who does not eat meat*

nectar *sweet liquid found in many flowers*

HOODED SEAL

The noses of male hooded seals can blow up like red balloons. Male seals use their red noses to threaten other males during the mating season. Hooded seals live in northern parts of the Atlantic Ocean.

STAR-NOSED MOLE

North American star-nosed moles have 25,000 sensory nerves on their noses. The moles' sensitive noses help them to find food in wetlands and marshes. While under water, these animals often blow bubbles from their noses and suck them back in. Scientists believe the bubbles trap smells to help moles sniff out their surroundings.

NAKED MOLE RAT

Is it an alien? Perhaps it's a baby squirrel. No, this **rodent** is called the naked mole rat. Its huge tusk-like front teeth are used for digging tunnels under ground. The mole rat lives under ground in the dark and is nearly blind. It feels its way through tunnels using tiny hairs on its body.

rodent *mammal with long front teeth used for gnawing*

DUCK-BILLED PLATYPUS

Australia's duck-billed platypus is one of the world's only poisonous mammals. The male has a claw-like spine on its ankle that carries **venom**. The platypus is also one of the few mammals in the world that lays eggs. This strange animal closes its eyes, ears and nostrils when it hunts and swims under water. The platypus hunts with its highly sensitive bill, which can easily detect the movements of nearby fish.

venom *poisonous liquid produced by some animals*

LOWLAND STREAKED TENREC

The lowland streaked tenrec looks like a hairy yellow and black mouse. But this tiny creature is actually more like a porcupine. It can defend itself with quills that detach and stick to predators. It can also rub special quills together to make a high-pitched noise that scares away predators. The tenrec is one of several animals found only in Madagascar.

AYE-AYE

Aye-ayes are some of the strangest-looking creatures in the world. They have large bat-like ears, bushy tails, long fingers and large eyes to see in the dark. Aye-ayes look so bizarre that some people in Madagascar believe the animals are a sign of bad luck. There are fewer than 10,000 of these odd creatures left in the world.

SLENDER LORIS

The slender loris was named after the Dutch word meaning "clown". It has giant eyes to help it see in the dark. In fact, the loris' eyes are so big that they take up as much room in the animal's skull as its brain! The loris lives only on the island of Sri Lanka.

PYGMY MARMOSET

The pygmy marmoset lives in South America and is the world's smallest monkey. It grows to only about the size of a human hand. However, it can leap up to 4.9 metres between rainforest trees!

EMPEROR TAMARIN

The South American emperor tamarin is a small species of monkey. It is supposedly named after Germany's former Emperor Wilhelm II. This is due to the tamarin's long white moustache. It looks very similar to Wilhelm II's moustache.

PINK FAIRY ARMADILLO

What is pink, weighs less than 0.5 kilograms, and moves through sand as if it were swimming in water? The pink fairy armadillo! This creature lives in Argentina. It easily moves through sand because its front feet work like shovels. The armadillo also has a tiny pointed head that helps it to burrow its way into small spaces.

CHAPTER 2
ODD OCEAN CREATURES

The world's oceans can be a dangerous place to live. Still, they are home to a huge variety of animals. Each ocean animal has unique traits and uses certain behaviours to survive – some of them are really bizarre!

GOBLIN SHARK

The goblin shark has been called "the ugliest living shark". Its long snout looks like a visor above its eyes. Nobody is sure what this long snout is for. Some scientists think the sharks use their snouts to detect electrical signals from other fish. When the goblin shark's mouth is open, it looks very much like a toothy goblin.

YETI CRAB

Yeti crabs are white and hairy and grow to about the size of a human hand. Scientists think the crabs' silky hairs may help to trap the bacteria that they eat. Yeti crabs live near **hydrothermal vents** on the ocean floor to stay warm.

hydrothermal vent *hot spring on the ocean floor*

BLUE SEA SLUG

The blue sea slug often floats on the surface of the ocean to find food. This creature is a master of disguise. One side of the slug is silvery grey to help it hide from sea creatures below. The other side of the slug's body is coloured blue to help it hide from birds in the air.

TRIPOD FISH

The tripod fish doesn't bother chasing after its prey. Instead, it props itself up on the ocean floor with three tall, stilt-like fins. Then it simply stands in place and waits for prey to come close enough to catch.

BLOBFISH

The blobfish has been called the world's most miserable-looking fish and was voted the world's ugliest animal. This fish looks just like its name – a big, ugly blob. Scientists believe this creature spends most of its time bobbing in the water waiting for food to float by.

HAIRY FROGFISH

The hairy frogfish attracts prey by wiggling a fleshy arm above its forehead like a fishing rod. This predator can stretch its mouth up to 12 times its normal size to swallow prey whole. These bizarre fish can also change colour to blend in with their surroundings.

PINK HANDFISH

The pink handfish of Tasmania walks on its fins instead of swimming. Its fins are shaped like human hands, which is how the fish got its name. These slow-moving fish are extremely rare. Only four of them have ever been found, and none have been seen since 1999.

RED-LIPPED BATFISH

Sometimes even fish seem to try to keep up with fashion trends. The red-lipped batfish, for example, looks like it has put on too much lipstick! The batfish lives near the Galapagos Islands and doesn't swim. Instead, it uses its back fins to "walk" across the ocean floor.

SQUAT LOBSTER

Squat lobsters look similar to lobsters, but are actually related to crabs. Their arms and claws often grow several times longer than their bodies. Some small types of squat lobsters on coral reefs in Australia look like colourful plastic toys.

DUMBO OCTOPUS

The tiny Dumbo octopus usually grows to only 20 to 25 centimetres tall. It was named after the two fins on top of its head. When it flaps its fins, it looks similar to the flying elephant from the animated film *Dumbo*.

GIANT ISOPODS

Some animals grow much bigger in deep oceans than on land. This effect is called deep sea gigantism. Most land isopods, such as woodlice, grow to only about 1.3 centimetres long. But giant isopods in deep seas can grow up to 38 centimetres long!

ANGLERFISH

The anglerfish could also be called the "angry fish". It always looks grumpy. But it got its name from the fleshy spine that sticks out from its head. This spine looks like a fishing rod and has a glowing tip to lure in prey.

BARRELEYE FISH

Some fish live so deep in the ocean that they're hardly ever seen. One of the strangest of these is the barreleye fish. Its barrel-shaped eyes are found inside its glowing, see-through head. It usually looks up through its head to watch for prey. But it can also roll its eyes forward to find and catch its food.

BIZARRE INSECTS AND BIRDS

The world is full of weird birds and insects. Whether it's flightless parrots, or worms that glow in the dark, you can find bizarre insects and birds no matter where you travel.

NAKED NECK CHICKEN

The Transylvanian naked neck chicken has a long neck with no feathers. It looks like a cross between a turkey and a chicken. People have even nicknamed it a "churkey" or "turken." The chicken's featherless neck helps it to stay cool in hot temperatures.

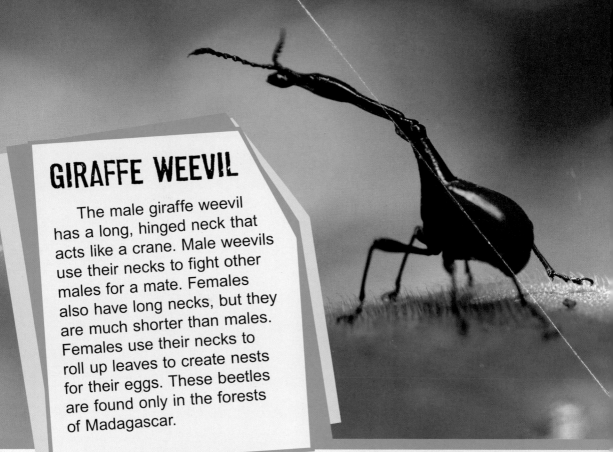

GIRAFFE WEEVIL

The male giraffe weevil has a long, hinged neck that acts like a crane. Male weevils use their necks to fight other males for a mate. Females also have long necks, but they are much shorter than males. Females use their necks to roll up leaves to create nests for their eggs. These beetles are found only in the forests of Madagascar.

ELEPHANT HAWK MOTH

The elephant hawk moth is found in northern regions of Europe and Asia and in North America. It is one of the fastest animals in the world. This big moth can fly up to 48 kilometres per hour! It can also hover and change direction quickly like a hummingbird. The caterpillar of this moth is long and grey like an elephant's trunk.

PANDA ANT

The panda ant is found in Chile. It looks like an ant dressed up in a panda suit. However, it's not really an ant at all. It's actually a type of black and white wingless wasp. Also known as "cow killer" ants, these wasps have painful stings. They are said to be powerful enough to kill a cow.

SHOEBILL

The shoebill is a giant African bird that can grow up to 1.2 metres tall. Its bill looks like a large shoe. Shoebills live mostly on land. However, they often build their 1-metre-wide nests on small islands or masses of floating plants. Shoebills can live for about 36 years.

NORTHERN SHRIKE

Northern shrikes look like harmless songbirds. However, they are fierce hunters and are often called "butcher birds". These birds kill more prey than they eat at one time. They often store the extra food for later. Sometimes they stab their prey onto thorns or barbed wire while it's still alive. Northern shrikes eat insects, small mammals and birds, and sometimes reptiles.

KAKAPO PARROT

The world's heaviest parrot weighs up to 4.1 kilograms and can't fly. Kakapo parrots climb trees and glide back to the ground. These colourful birds smell like honey because of a type of harmless bacteria that live on their feathers. The kakapo is found on only a few islands in New Zealand.

BOWERBIRD

Bowerbirds live in New Guinea and Australia. They make large nests called bowers out of sticks and twigs. Some bowerbird nests look like two tall, connected towers. Bowerbirds often decorate their nests with colourful objects. The satin bowerbird often uses brightly coloured rubbish and objects made of blue plastic in its nest.

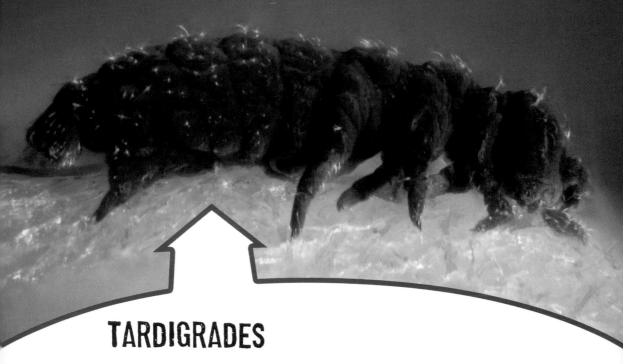

TARDIGRADES

Found all over the world, tardigrades are the ultimate survivors. These **microscopic** creatures are often called "water bears". Their bodies have tough outer coverings that help them to survive in even the most difficult conditions. These little creatures can live for years without water and can even survive in space!

microscopic *too small to be seen without a microscope*

ARMY ANTS

Army ants protect their queen and her eggs by creating **bivouacs**. The ants make these shelters by packing their bodies tightly together. Many species of army ants live in Central and South America. They are aggressive meat eaters. Army ants are known to form dangerous swarms to attack prey and predators.

bivouac *temporary shelter*

GLOW-WORMS

If you see thousands of glittering lights on a cave wall, it might be glow-worm **larvae**. Adult glow-worms create light to help attract mates. The larvae also glow, but they create light to attract and trap prey. They're often found in caves in Australia and New Zealand.

larvae *insects at the stage of development between an egg and an adult*

DRAGON-HEADED KATYDID

Borneo's dragon-headed katydid is the size of a large grasshopper. This colourful insect looks like it's wearing too much make-up. It has bulging blue eyes and a bright pink face. The katydid also has an extremely loud and high-pitched mating call.

CHAPTER 4
UNUSUAL ADAPTATIONS

From deserts to rainforests, there are many different habitats. Animals often make their homes in some of the toughest places on Earth. Animals in these locations have to adapt to survive. Some animals have gone through extreme changes, and may seem like strange creatures from another world.

MANED WOLF

The maned wolf of South America has very long, slender legs that help it to step over tall plants and grasses. The wolf also has 18-centimetre-long ears. The maned wolf may look large and frightening, but it's actually very timid. It eats a mixture of small animals and tropical plants such as bananas.

habitat *natural place and conditions in which an animal lives*

adapt *change in order to survive*

FOSSA

Would you like to run into a "killing machine"? That's what people in Madagascar call the fossa. These odd creatures have specialized feet and claws. They can easily climb up and down trees going head-first in either direction. This ability makes fossas excellent hunters. They eat mostly lemurs, rodents and reptiles. But they sometimes hunt farm animals such as chickens and goats. Although fossas look similar to cats, they are actually a type of mongoose.

SUN BEAR

The world's smallest bear lives in South-East Asia. An adult sun bear weighs only about 68 kilograms. The sun bear gets its name from the patch of gold or white hair on its chest. Some people think this patch resembles a rising sun. Sun bears have an especially long tongue that grows to nearly 25 centimetres long. They use their tongues to reach insects, grubs and honey inside trees.

GERENUK ANTELOPE

The gerenuk antelope can stand on two legs to eat! It does this to reach its long neck into trees to eat leaves and shoots. It gets all the moisture it needs from its food. The gerenuk can live its whole life without drinking water.

INDIA PURPLE FROG

Is a frog still a frog if it can't jump? The India purple frog has short back legs. Although it can move with long strides, it can't leap. This weird frog comes above ground for only 2 to 3 weeks a year during the mating season. It grows up to 7 centimetres long.

TADPOLE SHRIMP

Tadpole shrimp eggs can lie **dormant** in clay for years. The eggs hatch only when heavy rains finally come. The shrimp grow in the mud, lay new eggs and die within a few days of hatching. The new eggs will wait for the next big rains to hatch. Different types of tadpole shrimp are found all over the world.

dormant *not active*

THORNY DEVIL

Australia's thorny devil could easily be mistaken for a tiny dragon. This lizard's sharp spines are put to good use. The spines make it difficult for predators to swallow these lizards. Also, dew gathers on the spines at night so the lizard has water to drink. Thorny devils have spiny lumps on their backs that look like a second head. When threatened by a predator, the lizard ducks its head so only the spiny, false head is seen. The lizard's false head provides good protection from predators.

FENNEC FOX

The fennec fox is the smallest fox in the world. At only about 25 to 41 centimetres long – the fox is smaller than most pet cats. But this little fox has giant ears that grow up to 15 centimetres long. The fox's big ears help to keep it cool in the heat of Africa's Sahara Desert. Fennec foxes also have hairy feet that act like snowshoes to keep them from sinking into the sand.

ELECTRIC FISH

Electric fish live in freshwater lakes and rivers in Africa and South America. Electric fish send weak electrical pulses through the water to communicate with one another. Some of these fish can produce enough electricity to stun their prey. Electric eels, for example, can produce up to 600 volts of electricity. That's nearly three times as strong as the electricity in most homes!

GHARIAL

The gharial of India is one of the world's biggest crocodiles. It can reach up to 6 or 7 metres in length, which is longer than most cars! It has a round bulb on the tip of its narrow nose called a ghara. This bulb is used to make a very loud buzzing or hissing noise during the mating season.

DESERT JERBOA

The desert jerboa needs very little water. It can survive on the water found in its food. The jerboa has fur on the bottom of its feet to keep it from sinking into the sand. Like the fennec fox, the jerboa's large ears release heat to keep its body cool in the deserts of northern Africa.

AXOLOTL

The ocean isn't the only place where strange water animals live. The axolotl is an **amphibian** that lives in just one lake in Mexico. The axolotl spends its whole life in water. But unlike frogs or toads, it doesn't lose its gills or tail as it gets older.

amphibian *cold-blooded animal with a backbone; amphibians live in water when young and usually live on land as adults*

A WORLD OF WEIRD WILDLIFE

Some animals look odd or behave strangely. But they usually have good reasons for this. Being different can be a good thing. Unique traits often help animals to survive in the wild. Weird and bizarre animals are found all around us. Keep your eyes open – you never know when you might see one!

GLOSSARY

adapt change in order to survive

amphibian cold-blooded animal with a backbone; amphibians live in water when young and usually live on land as adults

bivouac temporary shelter

dormant not active

habitat natural place and conditions in which an animal lives

hydrothermal vent hot spring on the ocean floor

larvae insects at the stage of development between an egg and an adult

mammal warm-blooded animal that gives birth to live young and feeds them with milk

microscopic too small to be seen without a microscope

nectar sweet liquid found in many flowers

predator animal that hunts other animals for food

prey animal hunted by another animal for food

rodent mammal with long front teeth used for gnawing

vegetarian animal or person who does not eat meat

venom poisonous liquid produced by some animals

READ MORE

Animal Infographics, Chris Oxlade (Raintree, 2014)

Crazy Creepy Crawlies (Extreme Animals), Isabel Thomas (Raintree, 2013)

The World's Weirdest Animals, Clare Hibbert (Arcturus Publishing Ltd, 2011)

WEBSITES

www.bbc.co.uk/nature/animals/
Watch thousands of video clips of hundreds of different animals from mammals and birds to snails and slugs!

http://gowild.wwf.org.uk/
Find out about some of the world's weird and wonderful endangered animals. Watch videos, play games and take part in activities such as making an origami spectacled bear or a shoebox safari.

www.ngkids.co.uk/did-you-know/strange_sea_creatures
Meet some strange creatures of the deep, including the Christmas Tree Worm and the Wobbegong!

INDEX